PHOTO
FRAUDS

Keith Gaines

OXFORD
UNIVERSITY PRESS

Great Clarendon Street, Oxford OX2 6DP

Oxford University Press is a department of the University of Oxford.
It furthers the University's objective of excellence in research, scholarship,
and education by publishing worldwide in

Oxford New York

Auckland Bangkok Buenos Aires Cape Town Chennai
Dar es Salaam Delhi Hong Kong Istanbul Karachi Kolkata
Kuala Lumpur Madrid Melbourne Mexico City Mumbai Nairobi
São Paulo Shanghai Singapore Taipei Tokyo Toronto

with an associated company in Berlin

Oxford is a registered trade mark of Oxford University Press
in the UK and in certain other countries

© Keith Gaines 2002

The moral rights of the author have been asserted

Database right Oxford University Press (maker)

First published 2002

British Library Cataloguing in Publication Data

Data available

ISBN 0 19 917529 2

10 9 8 7 6 5 4 3 2 1

Inspection Pack (nine different titles)   ISBN 0 19 917535 7
Guided Reading Pack (six of the same title)   ISBN 0 19 917850 X
Class Pack ISBN 0 19 917536 5

Acknowledgements

The publisher would like to thank the following for permission to reproduce
photographs:

Brotherton Collection, Leeds University: p 16 (top); Camera Press: pp 10, 31;
Devonshire Collection, Chatsworth. By permission of the Duke of Devonshire
and the Chatsworth Settlement Trustees: p 4; Mary Evans Picture Library:
pp 6 (bottom), 21, 23 (top left), 28 (bottom middle and right), 29 (right); Fortean
Picture Library: p 13 (all); 14 (both), 15 (both); John Frost Newspapers: p 30 (both)
and back cover; Keith Gaines: p 3, 5 (bottom), 6 (top), 7 (top), 9 (both. Bottom photo
taken by Dr Robert Rines of the Academy of Applied Sciences, Massachusetts Institute of
Technology), 11 (all), 22 (both), 23 (main and bottom right), 24 (top), 25 (both), 26 (top),
27 (top, middle and bottom right), 28 (top and bottom left), 29 (left); Hulton Getty:
pp 8, 18, 24 (bottom); Science and Society Picture Library: pp 16 (bottom),
17 (both), 19 (all), 20, 26 (bottom), 27 (top, middle and bottom left); Martin Sookias:
title page.

Illustrations by Michael Ogden, David Russell and Thomas Sperling

Front Cover: Mary Evans Picture Library

Printed in Hong Kong

Contents

Fooling the eyes 4

UFOs 6

The Loch Ness monster 8

Bigfoot 12

The great fairy photo fraud 16

Glossary 31

Index 32

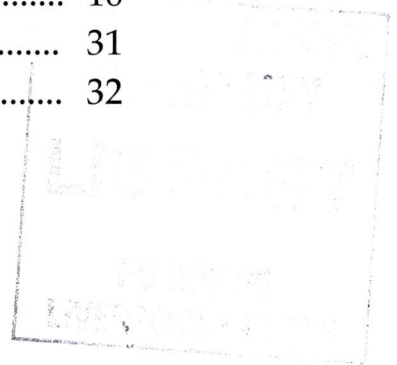

Fooling the eyes

Look at the picture below. It shows a violin hanging on a door. Or does it?

The truth is that nothing in this picture is real. The violin, the bow, and even the panels of the door are painted on a flat door!

This clever painting fools your eyes. Even when you stand in front of the door, and you know you are looking at a painting, it is hard to believe that you are not looking at a real violin.

This door was painted by Jan van der Vaart (1653–1727). It is in Chatsworth House, near Chesterfield.

Photographs and films show what is really there. Or do they?

The first photos were taken over 150 years ago. They were made by "fixing" images on flat plates that were sensitive to light.

Family photos were popular in Victorian times. It could take up to a minute to take a photograph. Special head frames helped to keep people sitting still.

People soon found that you can play with these images. You can put one on top of another. You can arrange things in a photo to make them look different to what they really are.

In this book we look at several photo **frauds**. They prove that you cannot always believe your eyes.

*A holiday postcard from 1931. This **fake** photo was made to make people laugh.*

UFOs

Hundreds of photos have been taken of **UFO**s. Many people say they are spacecraft from other planets. Most of these photos show fuzzy blobs that are a long way away. Many photos of UFOs really show balloons, helicopters or oddly shaped clouds.

UFO?

Earth

*A UFO follows **Gemini Twelve**, an American spacecraft, on 12 November 1966.*

Gemini Twelve

The photo (above) is from NASA, the American space organization. It shows what looks like a UFO, but it could be just some rubbish from the spacecraft itself.

Many UFOs are round and flat. They are sometimes called "flying saucers".

The picture on the right is quite clear. It shows a UFO unlike any other aircraft. It must be big because you can see its shadow on the ground (bottom right).

*Is this a real UFO? No, it is a **fake**. It is really a bit of silver foil on top of a real photo!* ▶

How to fake a UFO photo

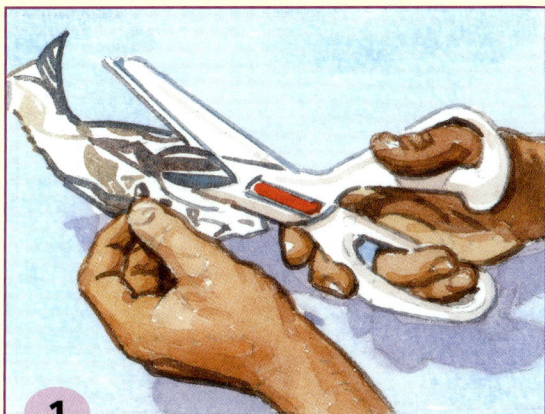

1 Cut a shape out of silver foil. Draw some lines and blobs on it.

2 Put the UFO on a real photo. Draw in the shadow.

3 Take a photo of your fake photo.

4 Sell your photo to a newspaper for lots of money!

The Loch Ness monster

Loch Ness is a big **loch** in Scotland. For years, people living around Loch Ness have reported seeing the head of a strange creature sticking up out of the water. Sometimes, there are humps in the water behind the head.

Photos and films have been taken of strange shapes and ripples in the water. These shapes and ripples could be made by a huge creature swimming in the loch.

This photo was taken in 1934. Is it the Loch Ness monster?

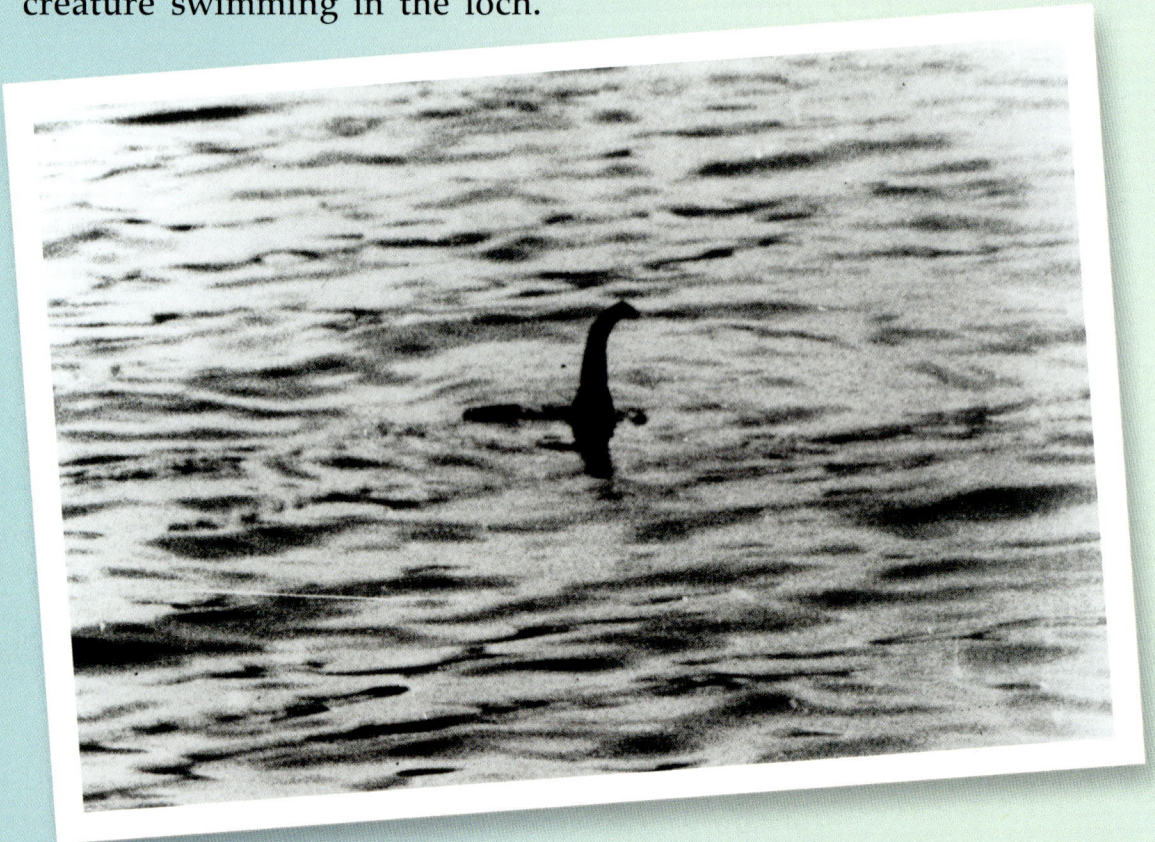

▼

For many years, the 1934 photo was the best proof of the monster. In 1994, the photo was shown to be a **fake**.

Today, the best evidence that something big is living in Loch Ness is a four-minute film. It was taken on 23 April 1960 by Tim Dinsdale. His film shows a hump in the water. The hump moves away from the camera, turns, speeds up, then seems to go under the water.

This picture is taken from Tim Dinsdale's film.

bank

loch

Something moves under the water.

Experts said that Dinsdale's film was not faked and that it showed something that was probably alive. However, like most photos of monsters and UFOs, the film is not clear enough to show detail.

This underwater photo, taken in 1975, shows the monster's head. Or is it just a tree root at the bottom of the loch?

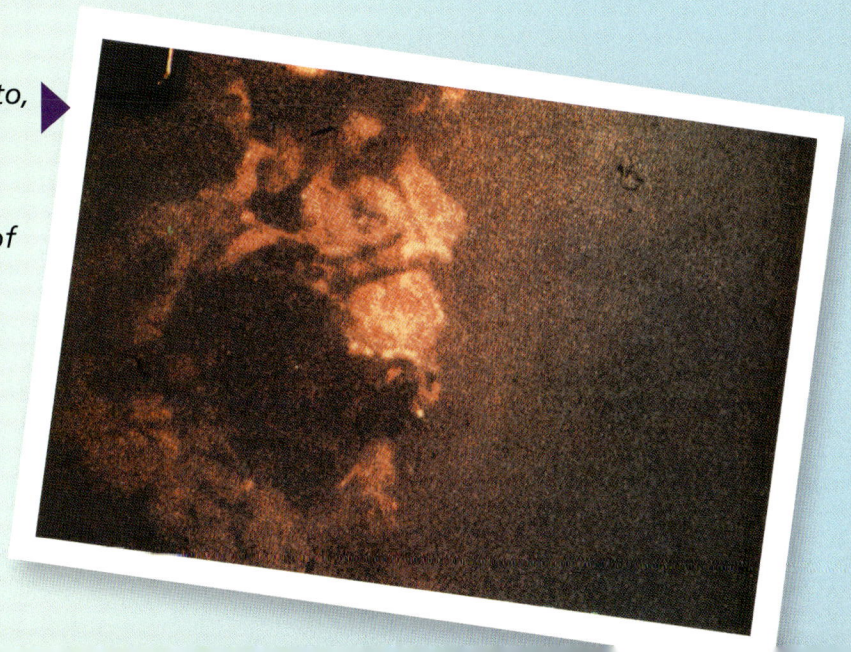

Mr H. L. Cockerell was a monster hunter. In 1958, he spent three nights in a canoe on Loch Ness. Near dawn, on the third night, he saw a huge head swimming towards him!

Mr Cockerell took this photo of what he saw.

Bravely, Mr Cockerell went closer to the monster – and found a long floating stick!

Mr Cockerell was an honest investigator. His photo was not a **fake**. He used his photo to show how natural objects, like sticks, rocks and even waves, can often look like "monsters".

How to fake a monster photo

1

First, scan both pictures into a computer.

2

On screen, cut out the head and neck from the dinosaur picture.

3

Paste the head and neck into the water photo. Put white splashes around the bottom of the neck and add some humps (from the dinosaur picture).

4

Cut out the bit with the "monster". Finally, clean up the photo, blur it, print it, then show everyone your photo of the Loch Ness monster!

Bigfoot

Over the last 150 years, there have been almost 1000 reports of a mysterious creature spotted in the woodlands of Northern California, USA. The creature is shaped like a man, but covered in fur, like a huge ape. Some people have also found huge footprints, so the creature is called "Bigfoot".

On 20 October 1967, Roger Patterson was riding his horse through the woods in Bluff Creek. According to Patterson, he saw a huge ape-like creature, over two metres tall, walking through the woods.

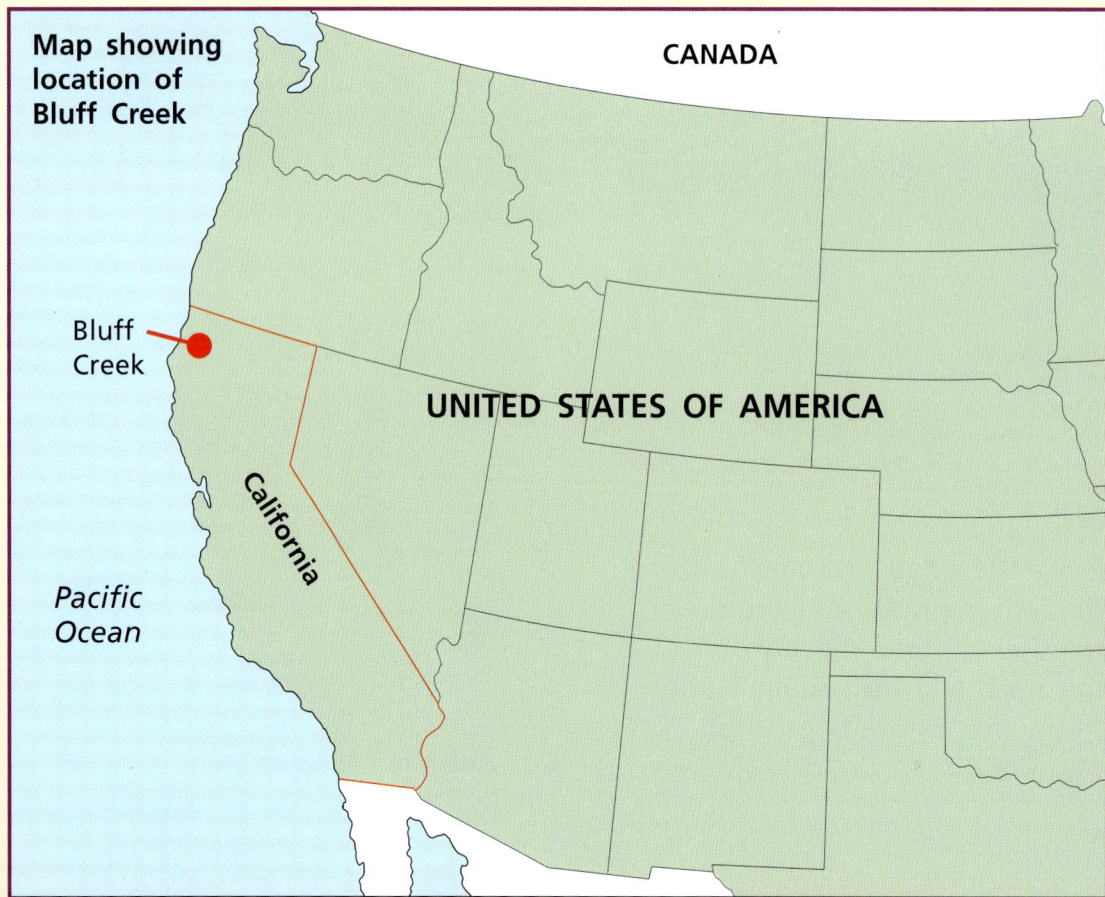

Map showing location of Bluff Creek

CANADA

Bluff Creek

UNITED STATES OF AMERICA

California

Pacific Ocean

Fame!

Patterson had a movie camera with him. He took 39 seconds of colour film of the creature.

*These **frames** of Bigfoot are from Patterson's film.*

Later, in a radio interview, Patterson said, "I was able to get some fairly good footage of it. It turned a couple of times and looked at me. And as it turned, it seemed to give the impression that it didn't want anything to do with me. It didn't run. It didn't act scared."

Patterson's film was shown all over the world. He became famous.

Many newspapers printed articles about Patterson's film.

The Times-Standard
Serving the North Coast since 1854
EUREKA, CALIFORNIA   SATURDAY, OCT. 21, 1967

Mrs. Bigfoot Is Filmed!

A YAKIMA, WASH, man and his Indian tracking aide come out of the wilds of northern Humboldt county yesterday to breathlessly report that they had seen and taken motion pictures of "a giant hominoid creature." In colloquial words they have seen Bigfoot!"

Thus, the long sought answer to the validity and reality of the stories about the makers of the unusually large tracks lie in the some 20 to 30 feet of colored film taken by a man who has been eight years himself seeking the answer.

And as Roger Patterson spoke to The Times-Standard last night, his film was already on its way by plane to his home town for processing while he was beside himself relating the chain of events.

Patterson, 34, has been eight years on the project. Last year he wrote a book, "Do Abominable Snowmen of America Really Exist?" This year he has been taking films of tracks and other evidence all over the Northwestern United States and Canada for a documentary.

He has over 50 tapes of interviews with persons who have reported these findings, and including talks with two or three persons who have reported seeing these giant creatures.

BOB GIMLIN, 36, and a quarter Apache Indian and also of Yakima, has been associated with Patterson for a year. Patterson has visited the area before and last month received word of the latest discovery of the giant footprints which have become legend.

Fake?

Many people said that the film was proof that Bigfoot really did exist and that it was some kind of ape. But other people said the film was a **fake**.

Roger Patterson said that he found footprints made by Bigfoot. He made casts of the footprints. ▶

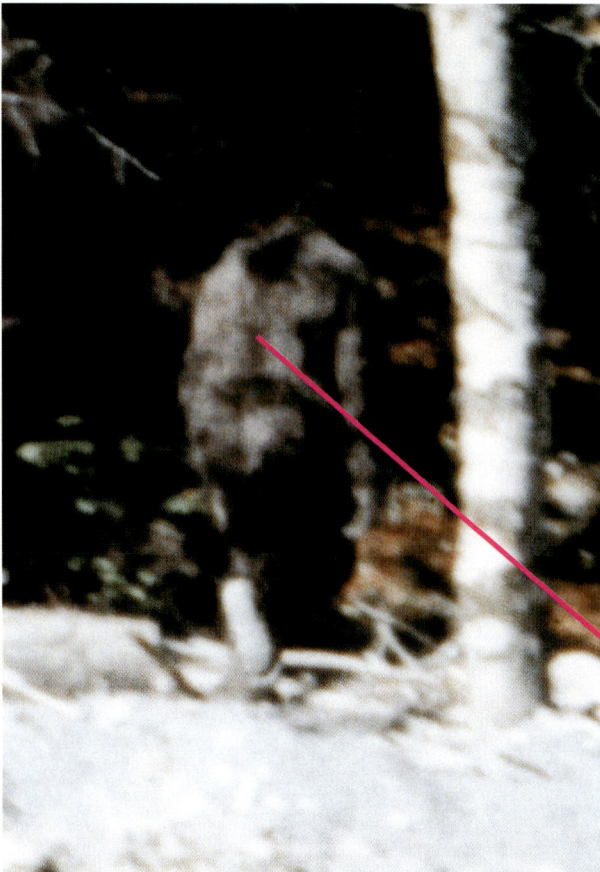

There were many things about the film and Patterson that people discussed:

- In the film, Bigfoot walked like a tall man, not like any known ape.

- There was a line running down the creature's back. Was it a natural line in the creature's fur or a zip in a gorilla costume?

A zip or a hair line?

Is this Bigfoot's footprint? The photo was taken by a forest worker the day after Patterson made his film.

This foot does not match the print.

- Patterson worked as a film cameraman. He knew some very tall actors. It would have been very easy for him to get hold of a gorilla costume.

- Patterson and many other people took photos of some huge footprints. Several pictures in the film show the creature's foot. Animal experts said the feet on the film could not have made the footprints in the photos!

Patterson died in 1972. Some people who knew him say he told them the film was a **fraud**. Most experts today are sure the creature in the film is not a "Bigfoot", but a tall actor in a gorilla costume!

The great fairy photo fraud

In 1917, two girls lived in a village in West Yorkshire called Cottingley. The girls were cousins. Frances Griffiths was nine and Elsie Wright was 16.

This photo shows Frances Griffiths (left) and Elsie Wright at Cottingley Beck.

Francis and Elsie were good friends who spent a lot of time together. Their favourite place was Cottingley Beck, a stream at the bottom of Frances' garden.

One afternoon in July, Elsie borrowed her father's camera and went down to the beck with Frances. Even for 1917, it was an old-fashioned camera. It did not take a film. It took only one photo at a time on a small piece of glass.

This is a "Midg" camera, the sort of camera that Elsie borrowed from her father.

When the girls came back, Elsie's father printed her first photo. He was puzzled. The photo showed Frances – and some dancing fairies!

The girls were pleased with the photo, but their parents thought it was some sort of trick.

Fairy photo 1

Frances and the fairies, taken by Elsie. Cottingley Beck is behind Frances on the left.

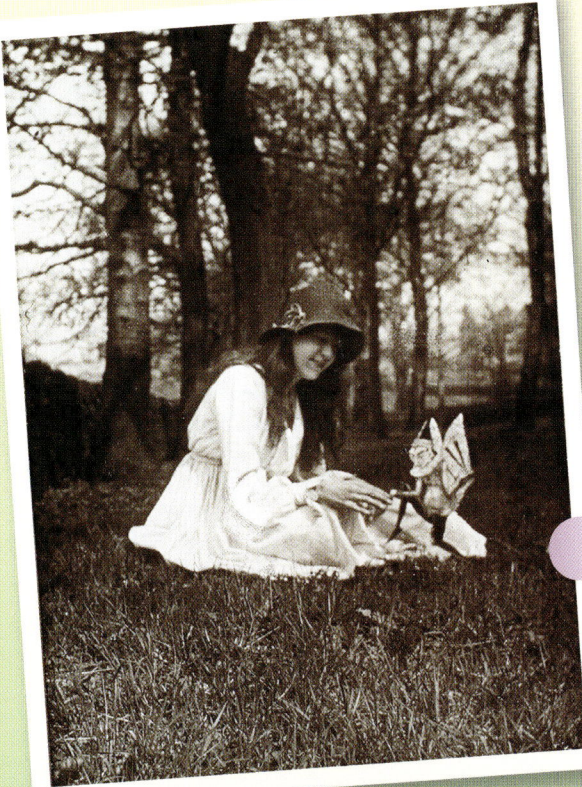

In September, the girls borrowed the camera again. This time, Frances took a photo of Elsie and a **gnome**! Mr Wright refused to lend his camera to the girls again.

Fairy photo 2

Elsie and the gnome, taken by Frances

Two years later, in 1919, the girls' mothers went to a meeting where a speaker gave a talk about fairies. After the meeting, Elsie's mother told the speaker about the fairy photos. He asked Elsie's mother to send him prints.

The two fairy photos were sent to London, where they were seen by many people. One of these people was the author, Sir Arthur Conan Doyle.

Doyle was writing about fairies for a Christmas edition of *The Strand* magazine. When he saw the fairy photos, he decided to include them in the magazine. But he wanted more proof.

Sir Arthur Conan Doyle was the author of the Sherlock Holmes *detective stories.*

Doyle had to go to Australia for a while, but he sent a friend to give the girls two good cameras and lots of glass plates.

On 19 August, the girls took two more photos. One photo showed Frances and a fairy that seemed to be leaping up to a branch. The other photo showed a fairy on a leaf. The fairy looked as if it was giving Elsie some flowers.

This is a "Cameo" camera. It is the sort of camera that Doyle sent to the girls.

Fairy photo 3

Frances and the leaping fairy

Fairy photo 4

Elsie and the flower fairy

Two days later, a fifth fairy photo was taken. It was not like the others. Neither Frances nor Elsie were in the photo.

It showed a small group of fairies. An "expert" on fairies said it was clear that the fairies were sun-bathing. The photo became known as "the Fairy Sunbath".

Fairy photo 5

The Fairy Sunbath. Both Elsie and Frances claimed to have taken this photo.

In December, the first two photos were printed in the Christmas edition of **The Strand**, with Conan Doyle's story about the girls. The newspapers reported great arguments over the photos.

"No one could have **faked** these photos," said one expert.

"The photos must have been faked," said a man from **Kodak**. Other people wrote to the newspapers, saying that they had seen fairies just like the ones in the photos!

It seems to us at this point that we must either believe in the almost incredible mystery of the fairy, or in the almost incredible wonder of faked photographs.

It is easier to believe in faked photographs than fairies.

On the evidence I have no hesitation in saying that these photographs could have been fake.

The day we kill Santa Claus with our statistics and our photographs, we shall have plunged a glorious world into deepest darkness.

◀ *Newspapers published different views on the fairy photos.*

People asked the two girls to take more fairy photos. They made several trips to the beck, but neither girl ever took another fairy photo.

The Evidence for Fairies
by A. CONAN DOYLE
WITH MORE FAIRY PHOTOGRAPHS

This article was written by Sir A. Conan Doyle before actual photographs of fairies were known to exist. His departure for Australia prevented him from revising the article in the new light which has so strikingly strengthened his case. We are glad to be able to set before our readers two new fairy photographs, taken by the same girls, but of more recent date than those which created so much discussion when they were published in our Christmas number, and of even greater interest and importance. They speak for themselves.

WE are accustomed to the idea of amphibious creatures who may dwell unseen and unknown in the depths of the waters, and then some day be spied sunning themselves upon a sandbank, whence they slip into the unseen once more. If such appearances were rare, and if it should so happen that some saw them more clearly than others, then a very pretty controversy would arise, for the sceptics would say, with every show of reason, "Our experience is that only land creatures live on the land, and we utterly refuse to believe in things which slip in and out of the

or lowering them, creatures could move from one side to the other of this line of material visibility, as the tortoise moves from the water to the land, returning for refuge to invisibility as the reptile scuttles back to the surf. This, of course, is supposition, but intelligent supposition based on the available evidence is the pioneer of science, and it may be that the actual solution will be found in this direction. I am alluding now, not to spirit return, where seventy years of close observation has given us some sort of certain and definite phenomena which have fairy and phantom phenomena which have been endorsed by so many ages, and still even in these material days seem to break

◀ *In March 1921, The Strand published another article by Doyle. It showed more fairy photos.*

For over 60 years, the Cottingley fairies remained a mystery. Were they real or faked? Before we learn the truth, let's look at a few of the things that were suspicious about the fairies in the photos.

Fairies here, fairies there, fairies everywhere!

There were fairies all around the two girls as they grew up. There may or may not have been real fairies, but there were lots of fairies in books, magazines and comics. There were fairies in adverts and fairies on posters. You could buy fairy cups and saucers, fairy wallpaper, fairy clothes, fairy cots for babies, fairy potties, and even fairy soap!

Fairies were often in children's comics.

COLMANS STARCH

AND AZURE BLUE

A fairy advertises starch, which was used to stiffen clothes.

These fairies represent the twelve hours. Dressed as pageboys, they are delivering invitations to a party.

A fairy advertises a meat paste.

Princess Mary's Gift Book

The year 1915 was the second year of the **Great War**. Many soldiers were killed. Often their wives and children had no money. Many other soldiers were wounded and could not work.

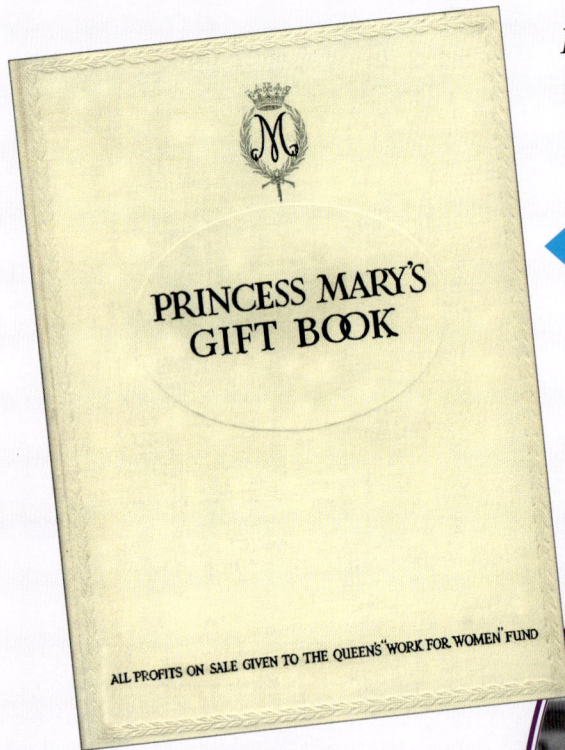

Princess Mary's Gift Book was sold in 1915 to raise money to help soldiers and their families.

PRINCESS MARY'S GIFT BOOK

ALL PROFITS ON SALE GIVEN TO THE QUEEN'S "WORK FOR WOMEN" FUND

This is the cover of Princess Mary's Gift Book.

Princess Mary

Princess Mary asked famous authors to write stories for the book. (One of them was Sir Arthur Conan Doyle.) Famous artists drew pictures to go with the stories.

Many children were given the book as a present, including Frances. It was one of her favourite books.

There was a poem in the book called "A Spell for a Fairy". It had a picture with it, of a little girl with fairies. It was painted by Claude A. Shepperson.

Another picture at the end of the poem showed three fairies dancing. The drawing was done two years before the first fairy photo.

◀ *The painting (left) and drawing (below) by Claude A. Shepperson* ▼

Look at the drawing closely
and compare it to
the fairies in
Fairy photo 1.

Can you see some similarities? They are not the same
fairies. Frances and Elsie did not cut out the fairies from
the book to **fake** the first fairy photo. But there are three
fairies in the photo whose legs are almost exactly the
same as the legs of the three fairies in the drawing!

Elsie was good at drawing and painting.
Did she draw the fairies in the photo?
Did she copy the legs from the book?

Turn this fairy a bit.
Its legs are the same
as the first fairy in
the drawing.

Turn this fairy.
Its legs are the same
as the second fairy
in the drawing.

Turn this fairy.
Its legs are the same
as the third fairy in
the drawing.

Fairies in fashion

Some people thought it odd that all the fairies had neat hair. Their hair was not only tidy – it was also cut in the same way as the hair of models and film stars of that time. Did fairies watch films? Did fairies do their hair like film stars?

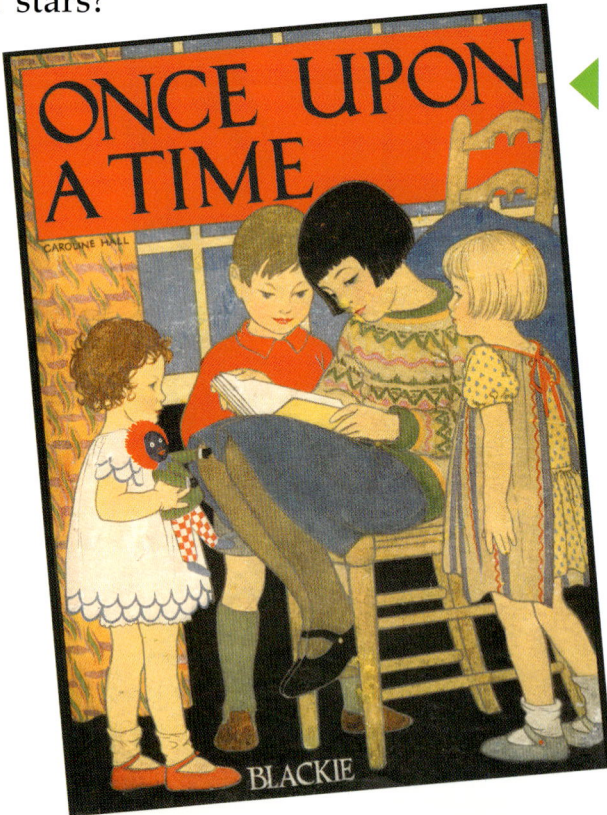

The older child on the cover of this children's book has neat hair. Her hair is cut in the up-to-date fashion of 1917.

The fairy in Fairy photo 4 has a very similar style of hair.

Was the fairy's hair copied from the book?

Odd gnomes

In the same children's book, there is a picture called
Fairy Chatter. It is very like Fairy photo 2, of Elsie and
the **gnome**.

In photo 2, the gnome stands in an odd way. Try it – you
will probably fall over! But the gnome in *Fairy Chatter*
stands in a similar way.

The gnome in Fairy Chatter

Fairy photo 2 shows a similar gnome.

There are other things that are alike in the two pictures.
The positions of Elsie and the gnome are almost the same
as the positions of the girl and the gnome in *Fairy Chatter*.
Both gnomes have a stiff pointed hat.

Did the girls read this book? Did *Fairy Chatter* help the
girls to take a photo of a gnome?

The truth at last

In 1983, when Frances was 81 years old, she spoke to reporters from *The Times* newspaper. She said that she and Elsie had not used any **trick photography**. What they did was simple, but it fooled everyone:

- Elsie copied some of the fairies from *Princess Mary's Gift Book.* She drew them on stiff paper.
- Elsie and Frances cut round the drawings.
- Then they made the fairies stand up by putting long **hat pins**, behind the cut-outs.

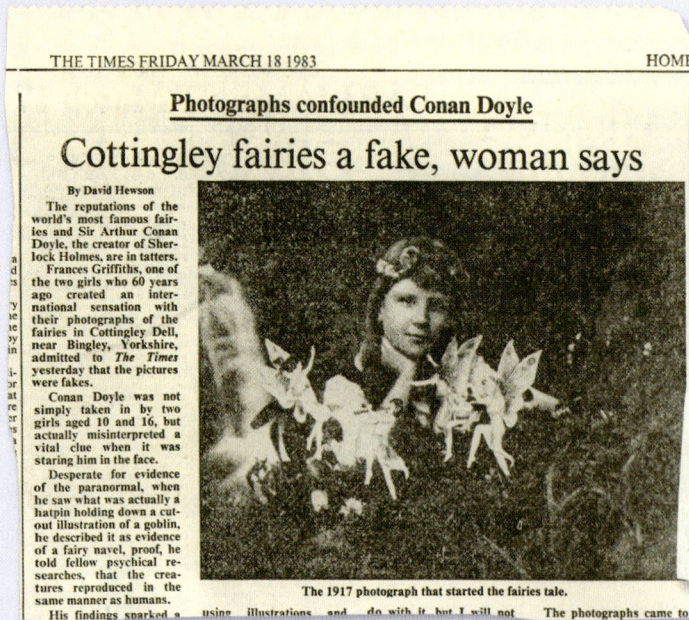

THE TIMES FRIDAY MARCH 18 1983   HOME

Photographs confounded Conan Doyle

Cottingley fairies a fake, woman says

By David Hewson

The reputations of the world's most famous fairies and Sir Arthur Conan Doyle, the creator of Sherlock Holmes, are in tatters.

Frances Griffiths, one of the two girls who 60 years ago created an international sensation with their photographs of the fairies in Cottingley Dell, near Bingley, Yorkshire, admitted to *The Times* yesterday that the pictures were fakes.

Conan Doyle was not simply taken in by two girls aged 10 and 16, but actually misinterpreted a vital clue when it was staring him in the face.

Desperate for evidence of the paranormal, when he saw what was actually a hatpin holding down a cut-out illustration of a goblin, he described it as evidence of a fairy navel, proof, he told fellow psychical researches, that the creatures reproduced in the same manner as humans.

His findings sparked a using illustrations and

The 1917 photograph that started the fairies tale.

More to discover about fairies

From Mr Geoffrey Crawley

Sir, In *The Times* on April 4 admissions by Mrs Elsie Hill were reported, that the 1917 and 1920 Cottingley Fairy photographs were fabrications in which she was partnered by her cousin Frances (née Griffiths), whose admissions had been reported in *The Times*, March 18. I feel that there are three points which should be made.

As regards Conan Doyle being "fooled", it should be pointed out that the basis for his belief was that a 15-year-old country girl, the first time she used a camera, could not have faked the first photograph – the one published with *The Times* reports.

Recently unearthed evidence

▲

Reports in The Times *newspaper, in 1983, reveal the truth about the Cottingley Fairies.*

The final mystery

Frances agreed that Fairy photo 1 was a **fake**. "What about the other four?" she was asked. "Are they fakes, too?"

"Three of them," said Frances. "But the last one's **genuine**!"

Glossary

fake (1) something which is not genuine

(2) to make something and pretend it is something else

frame one still picture taken from a moving film

fraud dishonest or false thing; a trick, often done to gain money

genuine something real, not altered

gnome legendary small creature, who lives underground or in toadstools

Great War the First World War, 1914 to 1918

hat pins long pins pushed through hats to hold them onto women's hair

Kodak American/British company making cameras, film and glass plates

loch large lake in Scotland

The Strand magazine which was very popular from around 1885 to 1925

trick photography changing a photo before or after it has been taken to add or take away something

UFO unidentified flying object thought to be from another planet

Is this the Loch Ness monster? This photo was taken in 1955 by P. A. Macnab. It shows something swimming near the castle ruins on the shores of Loch Ness.

Index

Bigfoot   12–15

Bluff Creek   12

cameras   7, 9, 13, 16, 17, 19

Cockerell, H. L.   10

computer   11

Conan Doyle, Sir Arthur   18, 19, 20, 21, 24

Cottingley Beck   16, 21

Dinsdale, Tim   9

fairies   17–23, 25–30

film   5, 8, 9, 13, 14, 15, 16

film stars   28

footprints   14, 15

Gemini Twelve   6

gnome   17, 29, 31

Kodak   21, 31

Loch Ness monster   8–11, 31

NASA   6

Patterson, Roger   12, 13, 14, 15

postcard   5

Princess Mary's Gift Book   24, 30

Shepperson, Claude A.   25

spacecraft   6

The Strand   18, 20, 21, 31

The Times   30

UFOs   6, 7, 31